Karen
2008

Read All About Sharks

SHARK FACTS

Lynn Stone

The Rourke Corporation, Inc.
Vero Beach, Florida 32964

© 1996 The Rourke Corporation, Inc.

All rights reserved. No part of this book may be reproduced or utilized in any form or by any means, electronic or mechanical including photocopying, recording or by any information storage and retrieval system without permission in writing from the publisher.

PHOTO CREDITS
©Marty Snyderman: cover, p.4, 10, 12, 15, 19, 20, 22; ©Doug Perrine: p.6, 7, 16; ©Tom Haight: p. 9; ©Tom Campbell: p.13; ©Mark Conlin, p.18

Library of Congress Cataloging-in-Publication Data

Stone, Lynn M.
  Shark facts / by Lynn M. Stone
    p. cm. — (Read all about sharks)
  Includes index.
  Summary: Presents simple information about the physical characteristics and behavior of various species of sharks.
  ISBN 0-86593-445-2 (alk. paper)
  1. Sharks—Juvenile literature. [1. Sharks.]
I. Title II. Series: Stone, Lynn M. Read all about sharks
QL638.9.S848 1996
597'.31—dc20   96-79658
                                                              CIP
                                                              AC

Printed in the USA

TABLE OF CONTENTS

Shark Size 5

Dangerous Sharks 6

Rare Sharks 8

Shark Birthdays 11

Shark Speed 12

The Shark's Friends 14

Shark Skin 17

Baby Sharks 18

Shark Cannibals 20

Glossary 23

Index 24

SHARK SIZE

Most kinds of sharks are not much larger than you. In fact, only 39 of 350 known **species** (SPEE sheez), or kinds, of sharks reach 10 feet in length. More than half of shark species are shorter than a yardstick.

The tiniest shark is the 10-inch long pygmy shark. The whale shark is the largest. It sometimes grows longer than 40 feet. The basking shark is nearly as big.

The great white shark is one of the largest sharks, reaching perhaps 30 feet in length.

DANGEROUS SHARKS

The largest of the "man-eating" sharks is the great white. It may reach nearly 30 feet in length.

Great whites have probably attacked people more often than any other kind of shark. The tiger shark, which can reach 20 feet in length, is second in the number of known attacks.

A watchful diver trails a large bull shark over a meadow of sea grass.

A 14-foot tiger shark prowls the shallow, grassy sea in the Bahama Islands.

The bull shark is another large, dangerous species. It has been found in the Upper Amazon River, some 2,000 miles from salt water.

Eighteen other species also are known to have bitten or killed people.

RARE SHARKS

Several kinds of sharks are very rare. They have been seen only once or twice.

The best known of the rare sharks is the megamouth. No one knew the fish existed until one was caught off Hawaii in 1976. Only one other has been caught since.

The megamouth is nearly 15 feet long. It has an enormous mouth with more than 100 rows of teeth. Scientists still don't know much about the megamouth's habits.

The rare megamouth shark dives off the coast of California.

SHARK BIRTHDAYS

Sharks are long-lived animals. Great white sharks probably live for at least 35 years and perhaps as many as 100. A Port Jackson shark was known to reach 25 years of age. Lemon sharks are known to have reached 75.

Sharks seem to be almost free of disease. That's one reason they are of great interest to scientists.

Sharks are bothered by small creatures called **parasites** (PEAR uh sites). The parasites don't help the shark, but they don't seem to cause it any serious harm.

The hammerhead shark (shown here) and its cousins often live a long time.

SHARK SPEED

Sharks don't spend their lives in high-speed chases of seals or smaller fish. Some kinds of sharks, just like old carpets, lay quietly hidden on ocean bottoms. Even the big sharks tend to cruise—at less than one mile per hour—rather than race.

The shortfin mako is the fastest of sharks, and one of the fastest fish in the sea.

The Port Jackson shark slowly prowls the ocean floor off the coast of Australia.

Some sharks are speedsters for short times. Blue sharks can briefly swim about 25 miles per hour. The shortfin mako is probably faster. It is one of the fastest of all fish.

THE SHARKS' FRIENDS

Big sharks are feared by many **marine** (MUH reen), or sea creatures, but not by the remora.

The remora, or sharksucker, is like a friend to a shark. The little, long-bodied remora fish attaches itself to sharks with its suction-cup mouth. It doesn't hurt the shark.

The remora lets go of the shark long enough to eat shark parasites. The sharks seem to sense that the remoras are helpful.

A bottom view shows the sucker-like underside of a remora's head.

SHARK SKIN

Shark skin is different from the skin of other fish. Fish with skeletons of bone, such as tuna, trout, and bass, have scaly skin. Sharks, which have skeletons of lightweight **cartilage** (KART el idj) have sandpapery skin.

Shark skin is covered by hard, tiny "teeth" called **denticles** (DENT uh culz). The rough skin helps a hungry, hunting shark to swim quietly.

Shark skin makes high quality leather after the denticles are removed.

Tiny "teeth," called denticles, give a sandpapery finish to shark skin.

BABY SHARKS

Many species of sharks bear their young alive, just as mammals do. Adult mammals, however, tend their young. A mother shark gives birth, then she swims away. A baby shark is on its own. If it's not careful, it may be a meal for a larger shark.

A newborn swell shark swims free of its egg case.

A horn shark laid this corkscrew-shaped egg case.

Some other sharks lay eggs. The young hatch from the eggs.

The whale shark's egg case is nearly 20 inches long. That's twice the length of an adult pygmy shark!

SHARK CANNIBALS

Certain sharks are **cannibals** (KAN uh bulz)—even before they are born! Inside their mothers, baby great white sharks, tiger sharks, and some other species, attack each other. The largest and most fit of the babies grow by eating their brothers and sisters.

Scientists believe that just two babies survive the fighting. One is born through each of the mother shark's two birth canals.

Long before becoming an adult, this great white shark survived by eating its brothers and sisters.

GLOSSARY

cannibals (Kan uh bulz) — animals that eat others of their kind

cartilage (KART el idj) — the strong, flexible body tissue that make up most of a shark's skeleton—and the ridge of a human nose

denticles (DENT uh culz) — the small, toothlike points found in the skin of sharks

marine (MUH reen) — of or relating to the ocean

parasite (PEAR uh site) — an animal that in some way lives upon another animal and causes harm to the host animal

species (SPEE sheez) — within a group of closely related animals, one certain kind, such as a *great hammerhead* shark

Remoras hitch a ride with a Caribbean reef shark.

INDEX

attacks   6
babies   18, 20
cannibals   20
cartilage   17
denticles   17
eggs   18
leather   17
parasites   11, 14
remora   14
sharks
  basking   5
  blue   13
  great white   11
  lemon   11
  megamouth   8
  Port Jackson   11
  pygmy   5, 19
  shortfin mako   12
  tiger   6, 20
  whale   5
size   5
skin   17
species   5